body story

CRASH

The Body
in Crisis

**BLACKBIRCH®
PRESS**

San Diego • Detroit • New York • San Francisco • Cleveland • New Haven, Conn. • Waterville, Maine • London • Munich

THOMSON
GALE

LIBRARY OF CONGRESS CATALOGING-IN-PUBLICATION DATA

Crash / Elaine Pascoe, book editor.
   p. cm. — (Body story)
Summary: Describes what happens when David and Laura are in a car accident and suffer serious injuries, ranging from a ruptured blood vessel near Laura's spleen to a major artery that burst in David's brain.
Includes bibliographical references and index.
  ISBN 1-4103-0062-5 (hbk. : alk. paper) — ISBN 1-4103-0183-4 (pbk. : alk. paper)
  1. Crash injuries—Juvenile literature. [1. Wounds and injuries. 2. Body, Human. 3. Accidents.] I. Pascoe, Elaine. II. Series.

RD96.6.C736 2004
617.1'028—dc22   2003012035

Printed in China
10 9 8 7 6 5 4 3 2 1

David and Laura's bodies are incredibly sophisticated. Each one is a finely balanced system of interdependent organs. But in their complexity lies vulnerability. As they are about to discover, damage to just one small part of this system can have dramatic consequences.

The human body is an incredibly complex but fragile system.

BRAIN POWER

Even during sleep, David is aware of the world around him. The sound of the alarm triggers electrical signals to fire towards a part of the brain that never sleeps: the brain stem. It is the on/off switch for consciousness, and it responds by sending a wake-up call to the sleeping parts of David's brain. A single signal ignites a huge area of the brain into life. Without this vital link, it would be impossible for David to wake up.

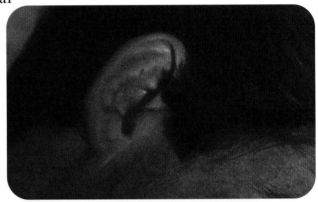

Right and below: During sleep, the brain stem takes control of the body completely.

What makes Laura and David unique is their brains. This single organ contains their thoughts and feelings—everything that makes them who they are.

Top: The specific wiring of each person's brain is what make him or her unique.

Middle: The skeleton and organs are vital to survival, but cannot function without instructions from the brain.

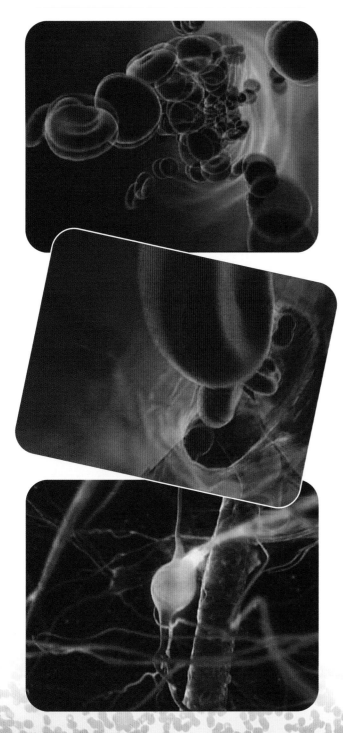

Laura's brain is connected to every organ in her body via a highly sophisticated life support system: the bloodstream. Every minute, Laura's blood makes a complete circuit of her body. It gathers oxygen from the lungs, and nutrients from organs like the liver. Even minor organs, like the spleen, play their part filtering out poisons so pure, oxygenated blood can be delivered to her brain. If this supply were to be interrupted for just three minutes, Laura would die.

Top: Vital nutrients travel through the body in the bloodstream.

Middle: The blood also carries wastes to organs that help to dispose of them.

Bottom: Signals from the brain keep essential body processes in motion.

THE ACCIDENT

Laura and David have been dating, and growing closer, for five months. On this morning, they are on their way to a friend's wedding. Laura is driving, and the wedding gift, a set of crystal glasses, is in the back of the car. But their lives are about to take an unexpected detour.

Crisis situations put the body in panic mode.

David calls ahead say they will be arriving in half an hour. As he chats on the phone, he suddenly sees danger straight ahead. He calls out in panic: "Laura!"

Laura's brain registers the danger. Her heart beats faster, pumping more blood into her brain. Her brain is speeding up, and time actually seems to slow down.

But her reactions are not fast enough to avoid the crash.

Top: Once it registers danger, the brain tells the body to react.

Middle: Danger messages are sent at lightning speed through the body.

Below: Despite warning messages, the body cannot react fast enough to avoid the accident.

On impact, Laura's spleen swings violently out of position, stretching the blood vessels that serve it. One vessel ruptures and starts to leak.

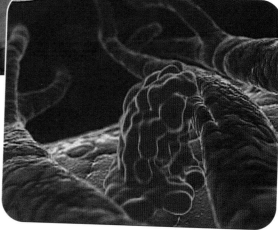

Top: The impact of the crash pulls Laura's organs violently out of position.

Top inset: Blood begins to leak from one of the spleen's vessels.

Below left: Laura's spleen is ruptured.

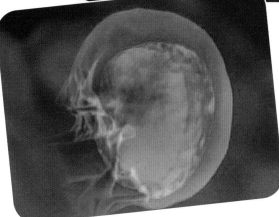

David's brain slams against his skull, severing connections and disrupting signals all the way down to his brain stem. His conscious brain is switched off.

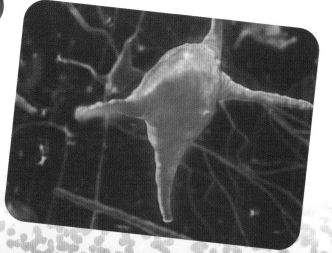

Top, middle, bottom:
Severe head trauma can destroy critical connections in the brain. These connections can control everything from speech, to memory, to breathing.

EMERGENCY RESPONSE

Laura regains consciousness in an ambulance, where paramedics are taking her blood pressure. Her first question is, "Where's David?" The paramedics assure her that he's OK, on his way to the hospital in a separate ambulance.

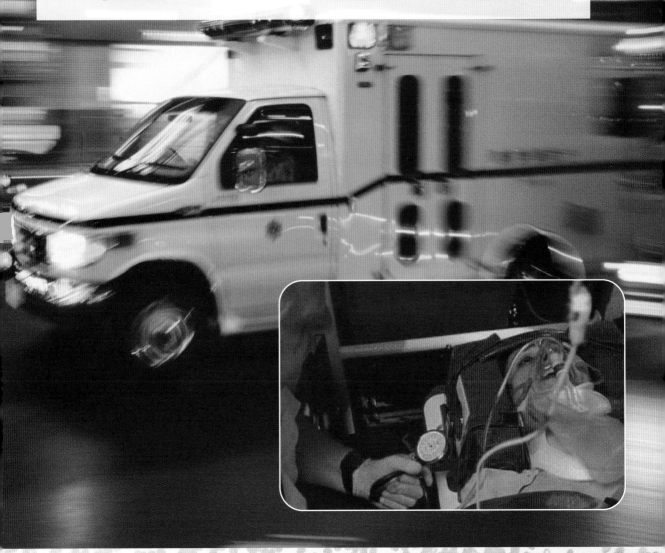

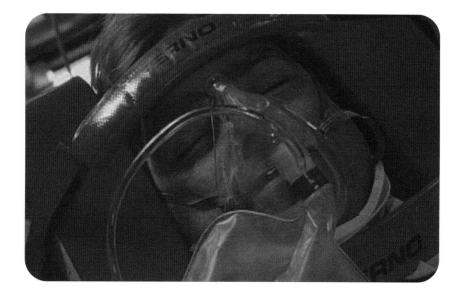

Laura does not know it, but David's condition is serious. He is still unconscious. Parts of his brain are shut down. The only reason he is alive is that the reflex centers of his brain, which control his breathing and heartbeat, survived the crash.

Top: The conscious part of David's brain has shut down.

Below left: The heart will continue to beat if the brain stem and reflex centers remain functional.

Below right: Vital signs are monitored in the ambulance.

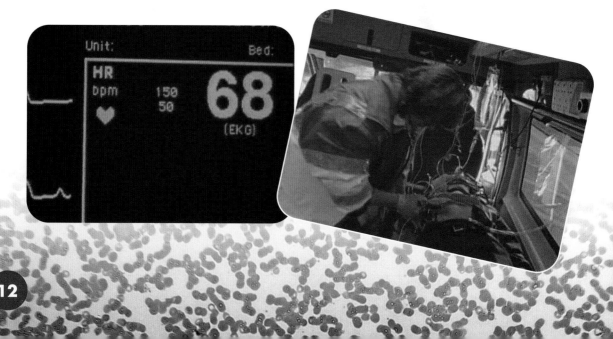

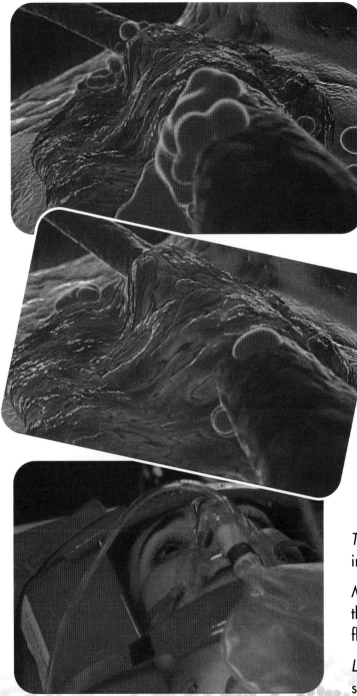

Laura is in better shape. Even before she reaches the hospital, her body is already at work repairing itself. The blood from the ruptured vessel feeding her spleen is congealing to form a clot, sealing the tear and stemming the flow of blood.

But as Laura's body heals, David's is getting much worse.

Top: Blood flows out of a rupture in a vessel.

Middle: A blood clot forms over the rupture and slows the blood flow.

Left: Laura's brain was not injured, so she remains conscious.

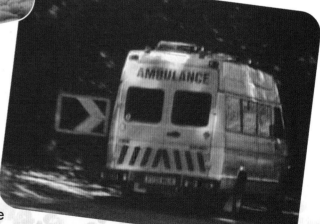

Under David's skull a major artery has burst, and the bleeding will not stop. Fresh blood is flowing from the damaged artery with such force that the congealing clot is simply pushed out of the way. The flow of blood squeezes David's brain, crushing the area responsible for his vital reflexes. His breathing falters, and his heart rate plummets. Unless the pressure can be relieved, and soon, the brain cells keeping him alive will die.

The ambulance picks up speed.

Top: An artery in David's brain has burst.

Middle: The flow of blood in the brain is so strong that it forces the clots to loosen and open.

Bottom: When there is bleeding in the brain, there is little time to take action.

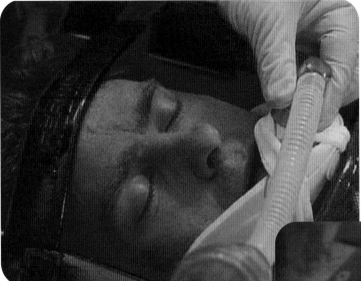

Internal bleeding in the brain creates increasing pressure, which squeezes the brain and makes it unable to function.

RUSHED TO SURGERY

At the hospital, the doctors are mystified at first. They do not know why David's vital signs are plummeting, and they do not have much time to find out. David is still bleeding, and in his skull the pressure is building—starving his brain cells of blood, quite literally squeezing him to death. But the cause is not obvious. All the bleeding is internal; there are no external signs. His airway is clear—yet without a respirator, he stops breathing.

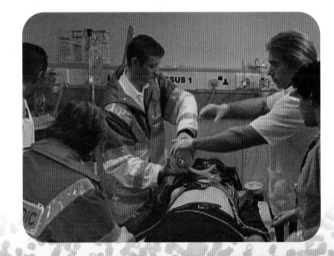

There is one vital clue. The pressure on his brain is crushing the nerves of his left eye, making his pupil dilate. Seeing that dilated pupil, the doctors guess that he has suffered a brain injury. Suddenly the stakes are higher, and there is only one thing to do. David is rushed to surgery.

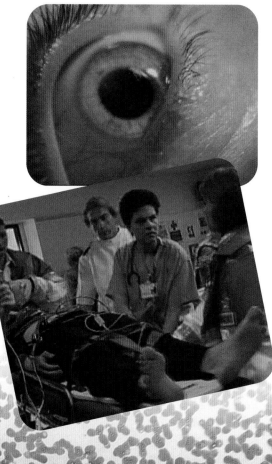

Top and middle: Increased pressure on the brain causes the eye's pupils to dilate, or become larger.

Bottom: Dilated pupils tell the doctors that emergency brain surgery is necessary.

The doctors know they must relieve the pressure inside David's skull quickly, or he will die. He is prepared for an emergency operation, and when his scalp is shaved, a bruise is revealed. That will help guide the neurosurgeons to the injury. But it is a delicate operation.

After the scalp is shaved, the surgeons can see where the injury is located.

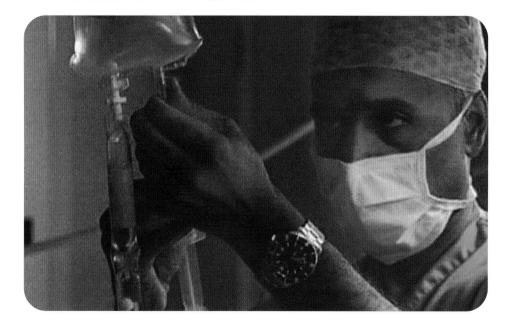

The doctors need to buy themselves more time, so they inject a drug called Mannitol into David's bloodstream through an intravenous drip. As the drug travels through the blood vessels of his brain, it draws out fluid—just enough to relieve some of the pressure on the brain cells that are keeping him alive.

Top: A drug called Mannitol is injected into the bloodstream.

Right: Inside the bloodstream the drug draws out fluid, which relieves the pressure somewhat.

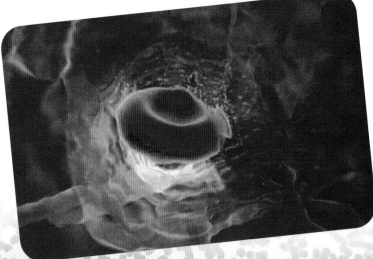

But only one thing can save David's life. The surgeons must open up his skull, remove the clot, and repair the damaged blood vessels. In the operating room, the surgeons drill a series of tiny holes in his skull. Then they break away the bone between the holes, opening up a 2-inch gap. Finally, the blood clot can be cleared away, and the ruptured blood vessels are sealed with heat.

The pressure is instantly relieved, and blood flows back to David's suffocating brain cells. The immediate threat to his life is over.

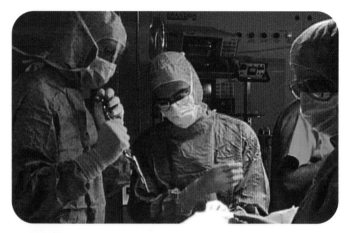

Right: The pressure on the brain can only be relieved by opening the skull and repairing the leaking blood vessels.

Below: As soon as the pressure is relieved, the brain cells regain blood flow and signals can once again flow.

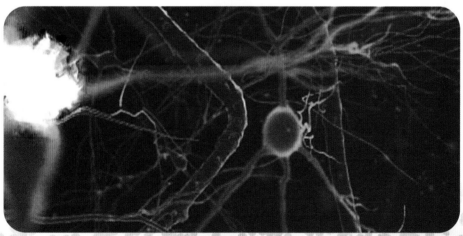

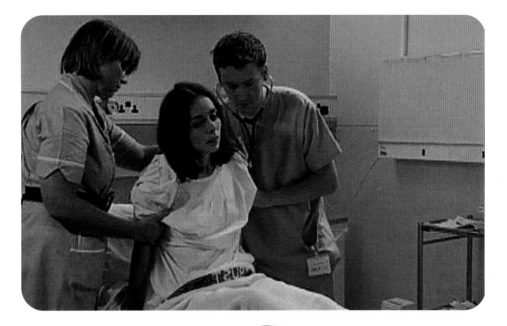

HIDDEN DANGER

Meanwhile, a team of doctors and nurses examine Laura. She is awake, alert, and still worried about David.

Laura's life does not appear to be in any immediate danger. The doctors order x-rays, and they want her to stay in the hospital for observation. But if her injuries are not too serious they will let her body repair itself.

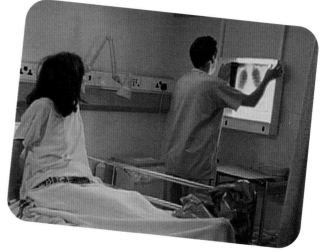

Top and above: Internal injuries for Laura seem to be minor. An x-ray shows only some swelling.

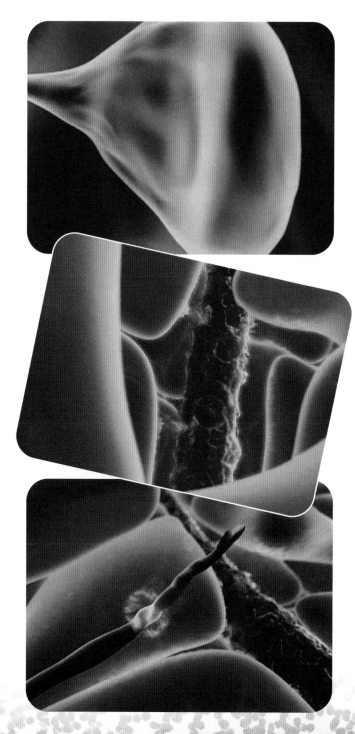

She is in some pain, but the pain she feels is actually part of her body's healing process. Within the protective membrane that encases the spleen, blood vessels are bringing fluids designed to heal Laura's injuries. As the fluids seep out, they cause the damaged area to swell, triggering pain receptors. The dull ache that Laura feels is a message from her body, telling her to lie down and give her injuries the time they need to repair.

Top: Fluids inside the spleen's membrane are brought by the blood vessels to help heal.

Middle: As fluid seeps out of the membrane, it causes swelling.

Bottom: Swelling causes pain receptors to become active.

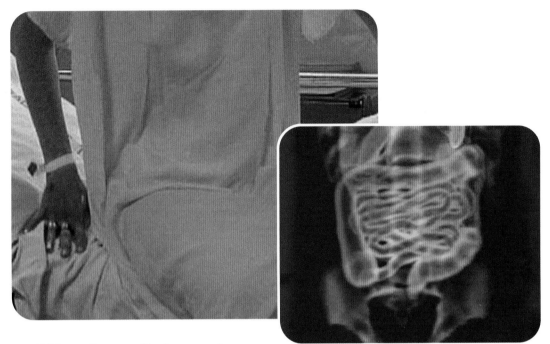

When Laura finds out that
David is unconscious and in intensive care following emergency
surgery, she is shocked. She insists on seeing him, even though the
doctors want her to stay quiet. Sudden movements could undo her
body's delicate repair. But Laura feels OK, and she promises to
take it easy.

Top and inset: Inside the body, delicate repairs and healing can become undone by too much activity.

Left: Body trauma also causes emotional trauma.

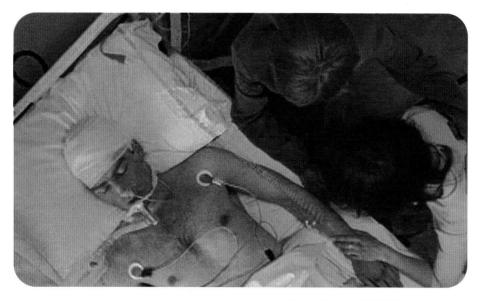

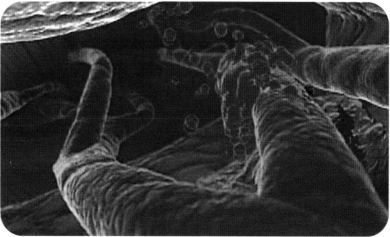

Right: A sudden movement causes a clot to break. Blood begins to flow out of the vessel and into the spleen's surrounding membrane.

But as she joins David's mother at his bedside, she does not realize that she has put her own life in danger. A sudden movement has broken the clot sealing her ruptured blood vessel. Once more, blood pours into the membrane around her spleen. If this keeps happening, blood will continue to build up until the membrane is stretched to the breaking point.

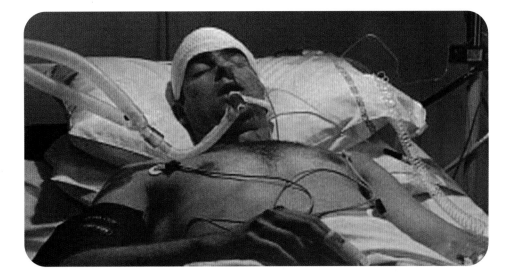

COMA

David's condition remains critical. Just as in Laura's spleen, healing fluids are seeping out of the blood vessels in his brain, making it swell so much that any sudden movement might be fatal. He is kept on a sedative drip to make sure he stays unconscious, until the doctors are certain that the danger is over. But David's chances of full recovery depend on how badly injured his brain is.

Top: Swelling in David's brain puts him in a dangerous situation. A sudden movement could be fatal.

Bottom: Fluids seeping from brain vessels cause immediate danger.

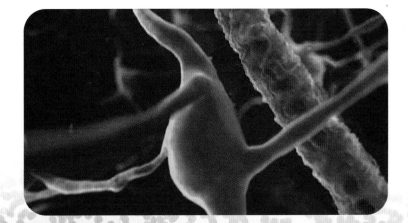

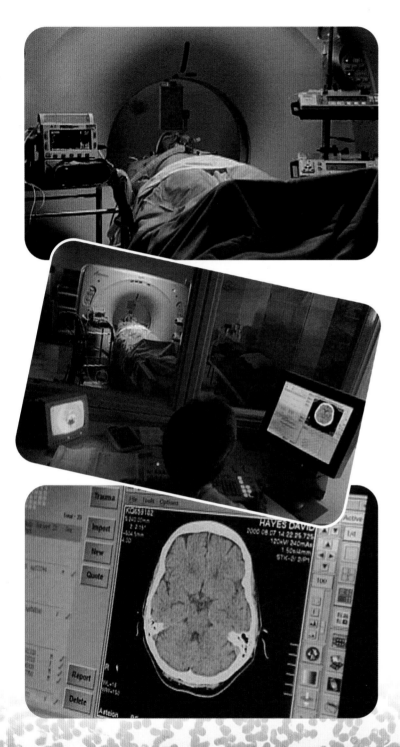

The next day, the news from the CT scan is good—the swelling has gone down, and there is no large-scale tissue damage. David can be safely taken off the sedative.

A CT scan—which is like a full-body x-ray —images the inside from many angles at once.

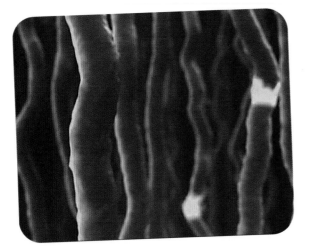

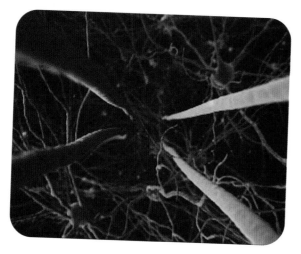

Top: When the brain stem sends signals to rouse the body, David starts to regain consciousness.

Above: Many connections in the brain stem were bent or twisted by the injuries.

But the scan cannot show the microscopic injuries caused by the impact. Some of David's brain cells are dead—they will never recover. The full extent of these injuries will not become clear until David regains consciousness.

As the sedative wears off, David's brain stem sends out signals to rouse his unconscious brain. He seems to be coming around, but there is a problem. Many of the connections leading from the brain stem were bent and twisted in the crash. Inside the connections, the delicate cell structure has been shattered. The signals get jammed. Because these signals cannot get through, most of David's brain remains switched off.

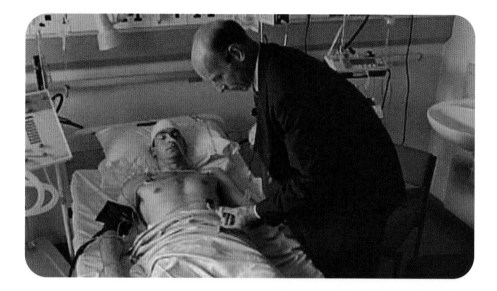

The nurse calls the doctor, who examines David, testing his responses to simple stimuli—verbal commands, light, and pain—to quickly assess which parts of his brain are working and which are not. The news is not good. David is in a coma.

Top, middle, bottom: Even though most of David's brain remains switched off, he may respond to certain stimuli.

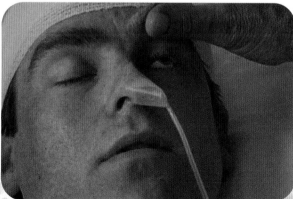

Even though it seems to Laura that he is trying to talk, he remains unconscious. In fact, a coma is rarely a state of total vegetation. Some areas of David's brain are awake, which is why he can make movements and noises. But that is about all.

The doctor says there is evidence that his brain is damaged, but it is too soon to tell if the damage will be permanent. It may be reversible, and the doctor is encouraged by the fact that David seems to be getting

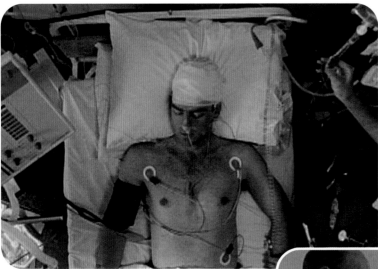

better all the time. Meanwhile, there is nothing to do but wait and see what happens. David's brain has to heal itself.

Top: A coma is largely a state of total inactivity.

Bottom: The doctor explains that David's brain is damaged, and his recovery is uncertain.

COMA

A coma renders a patient unconscious. While in a coma, the patient is in a sort of "sleep mode"—he or she is not awake or aware of the world around him or her, but the body continues to function. The most common cause of a coma is a severe brain injury. Such an injury, in turn, often cuts off or severely reduces the oxygen supply to the brain. Anoxia is what doctors call a complete absence of available oxygen. Hypoxia is what doctors call a situation where someone had available oxygen but at reduced levels for a period of time. Anoxemia describes when a person's blood supply (rather than lungs) lacks oxygen. Oxygen deprivation for longer than five to ten minutes can be fatal. Almost all patients that suffer five minutes or more of complete oxygen deprivation—or fifteen minutes of substantially reduced oxygen—sustain permanent brain damage. Those who do not end up in a coma typically have impaired learning ability and retrieval problems.

In general, doctors can tell a lot about how soon a patient will recover from a coma by what happens in the first twenty four hours after injury. If a patient does not show certain signs of recovery within the first twenty four hours, then after twenty four hours, the great majority of those individuals (87 percent) will either die or remain in a vegetative state and only 7 percent will wind up with a moderate disability or good recovery. Here are some other quick facts about comas:

- Most comas end with eye opening and regaining of consciousness; however 10 percent of patients who open their eyes fail to regain consciousness.

- Studies show that patients remaining in a vegetative state for at least one year after injury are unlikely to gain consciousness, although they may live for many years.

- Patients over forty years of age have a poorer rate of recovery than younger patients, post coma.

- Absence of eye opening in the first thirty days after injury is a sign that the patient is unlikely to recover.

- Patients who are apallic (open eyes, nonresponsive) can benefit from rehabilitation involving "sensory stimulation," such as hearing the voice of friends or family on a regular basis. Studies indicate these types of programs are helpful for patients who are at the boundary of coma and wakefulness.

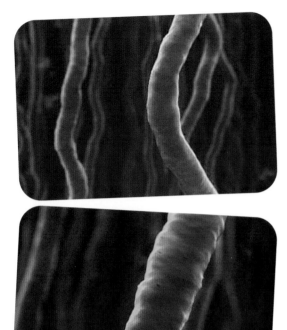

SLOW HEALING

And deep within the brain, the process of straightening the twisted connections has begun. Inside every damaged fiber the shattered structures are rebuilding themselves. But this process takes time.

Top: Slowly, the brain begins to straighten the twisted pathways.

Middle: As the fibers straighten, the connections increase and become strong.

Bottom: When enough fibers are straight, the brain will resume more normal functioning.

Laura continues to visit David, and she talks to him about family, friends, and anything else she can think of. Talking to coma victims can help to speed their recovery. In this case her familiar voice triggers David's brain stem into action, firing signals in an attempt to rouse the inactive parts of his brain. Even though the signals do not get through, it is possible that they accelerate the healing process.

Top, middle, bottom: Talking to coma victims can help to speed their recovery. Aural stimulation causes signals inside the brain to fire and improve their effectiveness.

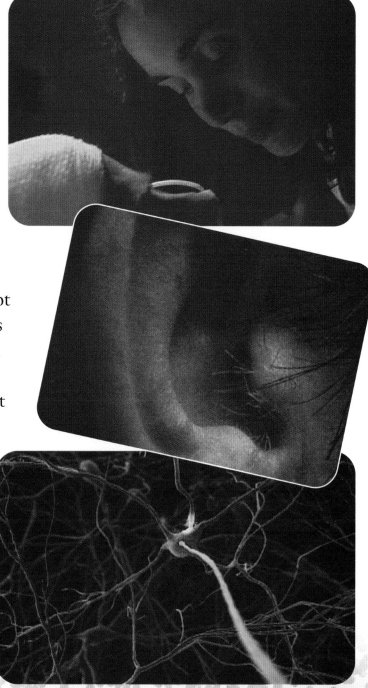

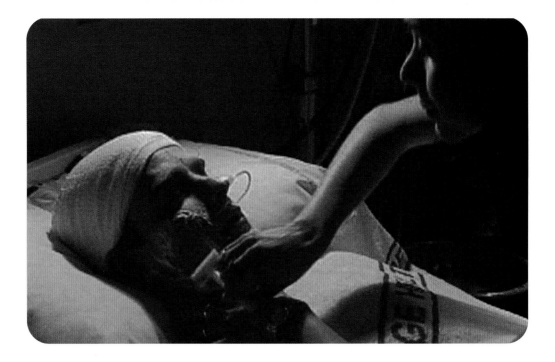

Laura is determined to be with David and help in any way she can. She is unaware that her internal wound keeps reopening. The membrane around her spleen is filling up with blood. She feels nothing but a dull ache in her side.

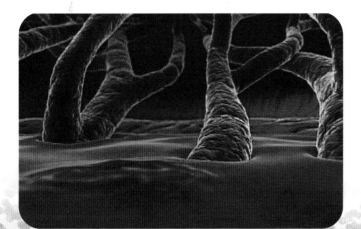

Top: Laura spends time with David while he remains unconscious.

Bottom: The membrane around Laura's spleen continues to fill with blood.

Eight days after the accident, David's brain stem finally makes contact with the rest of his brain. The nerve fibers carrying the signals have successfully repaired themselves. Circuits are ignited deep in his unconscious brain. For the first time in more than a week David is waking up.

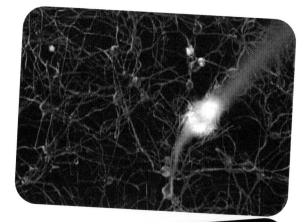

Top, middle, bottom: After the nerve fibers in the brain have repaired themselves, enough signals flow to spark consciouness once again.

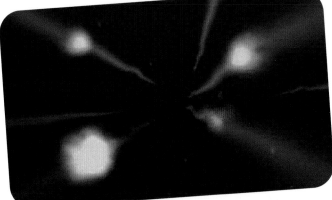

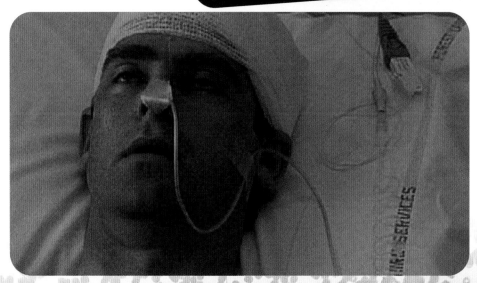

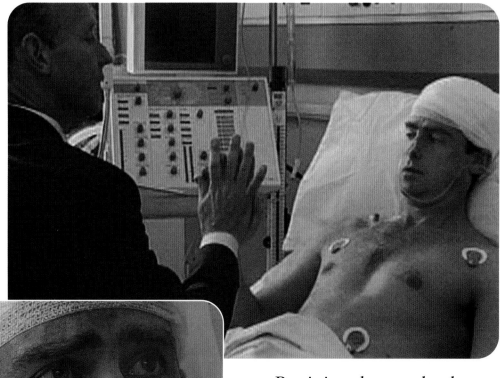

Above: Once consciouness is regained, a full assessment of brain damage can be done.

But it is only now that he is conscious that the full extent of the damage to his brain is revealed. The blow to his head severed millions of connections in his brain, and many signals cannot get through. He is having trouble moving his right arm and has lost the use of his right hand. And there is another, less visible problem. He has no memory of the past year. When Laura arrives, he does not recognize her.

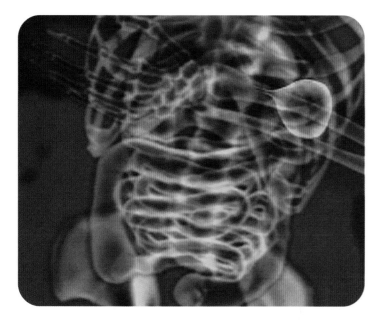

NEW HOPE— AND DANGER

Ten days after the crash the ache in Laura's side is getting worse, but she does not realize the danger that this pain represents. Blood has continued to leak from her broken vessel. What was once a membrane encasing her spleen is now a bloated, blood-filled sac. Laura needs urgent medical attention, and if she does not get it soon, the consequences could be catastrophic.

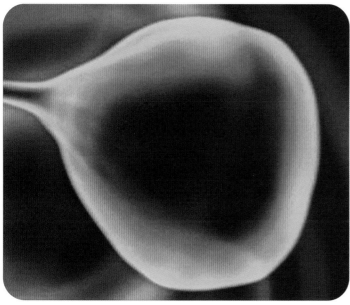

Top: Inside Laura's body, the spleen injury worsens.

Bottom: The membrane around her spleen becomes a bloated sac.

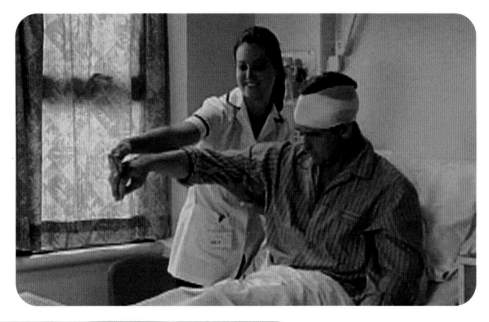

Above: Physical therapy encourages new brain connections to form. These new connections can replace ones that were destroyed by injury.

David, however, continues to improve. In the forty eight hours since he regained consciousness, the job of fixing his hand has begun. When his muscles are exercised in physical therapy, signals fire up his spine into the damaged part of his brain—stimulating the growth of new connections to take on the role from the ones he has lost.

David's brain is rewiring itself to regain control of his hand. Unfortunately, no amount of medical intervention will help David regain his lost memory. Unlike physical skills, memories do not exist in any one place in the brain. No one knows exactly where they are stored, but every connection in the brain may be involved in some way. A break to any one connection can mean loss of a whole range of memories.

Below: Memory loss is also caused by broken or damaged brain circuitry. The only way to regain lost memories is for the brain to repair itself.

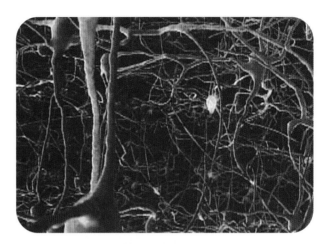

For David, the five months he has known Laura are a total blank. She tries to jog his memory with photos and conversation, but he only remembers people and things he has known a long time. Older memories, such as the face of a lifelong friend, are imprinted in strong, well-established circuits. But newer memories, such as a recent event, are less well stored. They are more vulnerable to loss, and harder to recall.

At this point, no one can tell how much of David's memory he will recover.

Top, middle, bottom: Short-term memory is the most vulnerable to loss by injury.

LAURA'S COLLAPSE

Laura, meanwhile, is on the brink of disaster. Her blood-filled sac is now stretched to breaking point. It explodes, ripping the top of Laura's spleen. All she feels is a stab of pain. But a massive trauma has just been unleashed in her body.

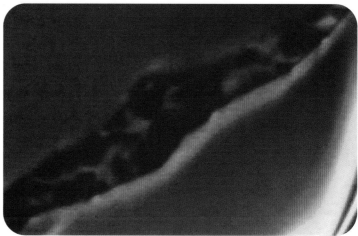

Above: As the sac surrounding the spleen reaches capacity, it bursts open, causing immediate and life-threatening pain.

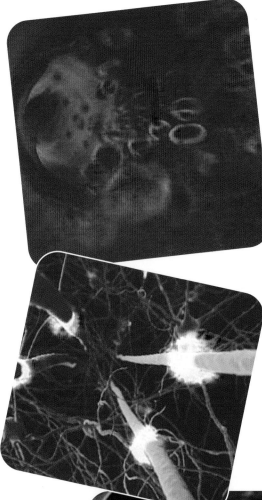

Laura's body is in crisis. A third of her blood supply has poured into her belly. In an effort to get more blood to her brain, her heart beats faster. But the faster it beats, the faster blood pumps out of her shattered spleen.

Laura's brain is being starved of life-giving blood. In a last effort to keep her alive, her brain stem acts. It starts to shut down every part of her brain not vital to survival. She collapses.

Top: Blood pours into Laura's belly.

Middle: Starved for blood, Laura's brain shuts down all nonvital functions and she loses consciousness (bottom).

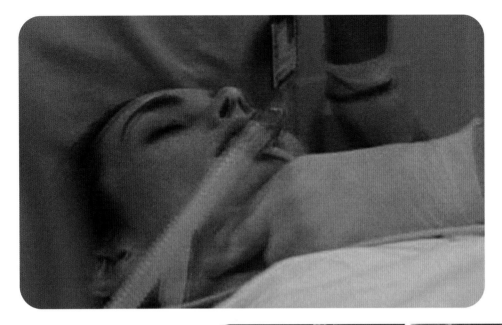

Laura's body is fighting a losing battle. If the source of her bleeding cannot be found and stopped in the next few minutes, she will die. All the blood her body can spare is being diverted to the reflex center of her brain. But there is barely enough to keep the cells going. Every drop of blood lost into her belly loosens Laura's grip on life a little more.

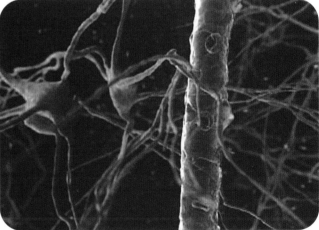

Above: Laura will remain unconscious as her brain slowly shuts down. Signals are fewer and farther between.

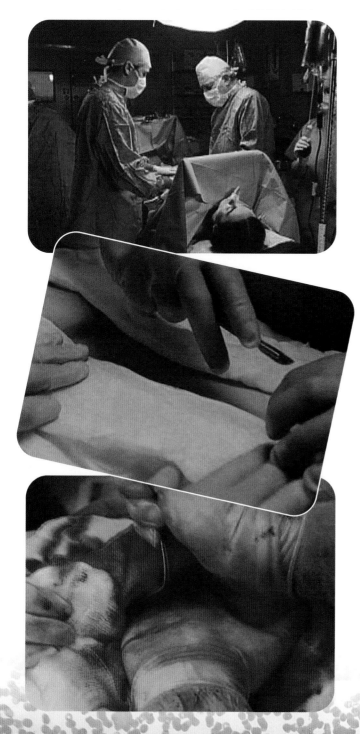

As she is rushed into surgery, the only thing keeping Laura alive is the blood being been pumped into her.

An enormous lake of blood has built up inside her belly. As the dam bursts, she bleeds out faster than ever, draining blood from her brain. The surgeon has only moments to find and repair the damage. But there is so much blood that he is forced to work blind. His only hope is to locate the rupture by touch.

Top, middle, bottom: Emergency surgery is needed to find the ruptured vessels and repair them before too much blood is lost.

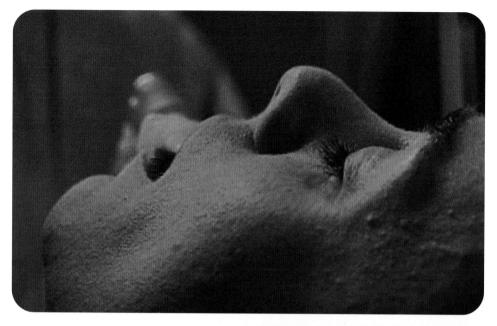

And he does—he finds the site and clamps the artery leading to the spleen, stemming the blood loss. Within seconds, blood starts to flow back to Laura's brain. Her chances of surviving have just risen dramatically.

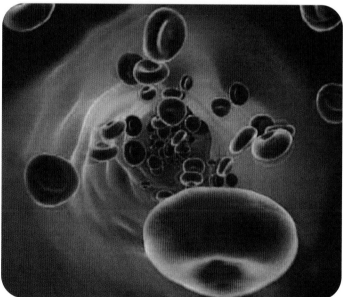

As blood flow returns to the brain, Laura's body begins to recover.

Now the surgeon can get a proper look at her damaged spleen. He needs to determine if the spleen should be removed, which would weaken Laura's immune system and require her to take antibiotics for the rest of her life.

It looks like about 60 percent of the organ can be saved, but trying to repair it is a tricky operation. First, the damaged section is removed. The remainder is sewn up. Then comes the moment of truth—the clamp is taken off the artery, and blood flows back into the spleen.

The seal holds. The operation is a success. Laura's spleen and life have been saved.

Top: The damaged spleen is assessed and part of it is removed. The remainder is sewn up.

Bottom: If the seal holds, the spleen will function once again.

THE SPLEEN

The spleen is part of the body's blood-cleansing system, also called the lymphatic system. The lymphatic network is an extensive drainage system that returns water and proteins from various tissues back to the bloodstream. It is made up of a complex of ducts, called lymph vessels that carry lymph, a clear, watery fluid that resembles the plasma of blood. Wherever there are blood vessels in the body, there are lymph vessels, and the two systems work together.

The lymphatic system returns fluid from body tissues to the blood. If excess fluid is not returned to the blood, the body's tissues become swollen. When a body part swells, for example, it may be because there is too much fluid in the tissues in that area. The lymph vessels collect that excess fluid and carry it to the veins through the lymphatic system.

The lymphatic system also helps defend the body against invasion by disease-causing agents such as viruses, bacteria, or fungi. Harmful foreign materials are filtered out by small masses of tissue called lymph nodes that lie along the network of lymphatic vessels. These nodes house lymphocytes (white blood cells), some of which produce antibodies. The antibodies are special proteins that fight off infection. They also stop infections from spreading through the body by trapping disease-causing germs and destroying them.

The spleen plays a key role in cleansing the body's blood on a regular basis. Red blood cells (manufactured in the bone marrow) are continuously being produced and broken down. They live for approximately 120 days in the circulatory system before they are eventually removed by the spleen. Platelets are also made in the bone marrow. They survive in the circulatory system for an average of 9–10 days before being removed from the body by the spleen.

The spleen also plays an important part in a person's immune system and helps the body fight infection. Like the lymph nodes, the spleen contains antibody-producing lymphocytes. These antibodies weaken or kill bacteria, viruses, and other organisms that cause infection. Also, if the blood passing through the spleen carries damaged cells, white blood cells called macrophages in the spleen will destroy them and clear them from the bloodstream. The spleen is the largest single mass of lymphoid tissue in the body. .

RECOVERY

Twelve hours after her operation, Laura's sedative is wears off. She wakes up to see David at her side. And this time, he remembers her.

David and Laura owe their lives to surgery. But without their bodies' ability to prolong life to the last, the doctors' efforts would have been in vain. Ultimately, it is the body's remarkable capacity to heal that will allow their full recovery.

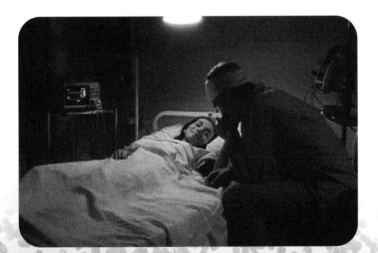

Above: Successful surgery means that both David and Laura will survive as their bodies finish the healing process on their own.

Left: David's and Laura's bodies have been through major trauma.

GLOSSARY

anoxemia The condition of having too little oxygen in the blood.

anoxia The condition of having very little or no oxygen in the tissues.

antibodies Proteins that fight off infection; part of the immune system.

apallic A state of coma in which the eyes are open but the person is nonresponsive.

artery A vessel that carries blood from the heart through the body.

bloodstream The network of arteries, veins, and blood that moves oxygen and nutrients through the body.

brain stem The portion of the brain that connects the spinal cord to the forebrain and controls consciousness.

clot A mass of coagulated or concentrated blood.

coma A state of profound unconsciousness caused by injury or disease.

CT scan Computerized tomography, a way for doctors to see the inside of the body.

dilate To expand or widen.

hypoxia The condition of having a less than desirable amount of oxygen in the tissues.

lymph A pale fluid that removes bacteria and certain proteins from tissues.

lymphatic system The network of lymph, lymph nodes, and lymph vessels that helps clean the blood.

lymph nodes A round mass of lymphoid tissue.

lymphocytes White blood cells.

mannitol A drug used to draw excess fluids out of the body.

neurosurgeon A doctor who practices surgery on the nervous system such as nerves, brain, and spinal cord.

platelets Flat disks of blood that aid in clotting.

sedative A drug that calms or tranquilizes.

spleen An organ that helps to filter blood.

INDEX

j617.102 Crash.
CRA

$23.70   259480